THE CURIOU

"A witty and accessible treasure trove of scientific discoveries that goes to the heart of our human quest to understand who we are. This book doesn't dumb down or gloss over imponderables but will leave you marvelling at the science and asking for more."

PROFESSOR REBECCA FITZGERALD
Director of Medical Studies, University of Cambridge
Lister Prize Fellowship (2008), NHS Innovation (2011), NIHR
Research Professorship (2013)

"Has the bug bitten you? Are you curious? Curious to know how the universe evolved from the Big Bang? How matter arranges itself into objects ranging from atomic nuclei to human beings, planets,and stars? Are you curious to know why all these things are the way they are?

Science is good for the 'how' questions but does not necessarily have the answers on the 'why' questions. Can science and religion talk to each other? Enjoy this series and learn more about science and the enriching dialogue between science and faith."

PROFESSOR ROLF HEUER
Director General of CERN from 2009 to 2015
President of the German Physical Society and President of the
SESAME Council

"Here is a wonderful and wittily written introduction to science as the art of asking open questions and not jumping to conclusions. It's also an amusing excursion through evolution and anthropology which packs in a lot of learning with the lightest of touches. A much-needed antidote to the bludgeoning crudity of so much writing in both science and religion."

REVEREND DOCTOR MALCOLM GUITE
Poet, singer-songwriter, priest, and academic
Chaplain at Girton College Cambridge

THE CURIOUS SCIENCE QUEST

VICTORIAN VOYAGES

WHERE DID WE COME FROM?

JULIA GOLDING

WITH ANDREW BRIGGS AND ROGER WAGNER

ILLUSTRATIONS BRETT HUDSON

LION
CHILDREN'S

Published by Lion Children's Books
an imprint of
Lion Hudson Limited
Wilkinson House, Jordan Hill Business Park, Banbury Road,
Oxford OX2 8DR, England
www.lionhudson.com/lionchildrens
ISBN 978 0 7459 7754 6
e-ISBN 978 07459 7801 7

First edition 2019

Acknowledgments
This publication was made possible through the support of a grant from
Templeton Religion Trust. The opinions expressed in this publication are those
of the authors and do not necessarily reflect the views of Templeton Religion
Trust.

A catalogue record for this book is available from the British Library

Printed and bound in the UK, May 2019, LH26

CONTENTS

INTRODUCTION

Life is full of big questions, what we might call ultimate questions. In the first four parts of the Curious Science Quest our intrepid time travellers, Harriet and Milton, explored four of the most important mysteries:

- When did humans start to ask questions?
- Who were the first scientists?
- What is our place in the solar system?
- What are the laws of the universe?

STOP BUGGING ME!

They have met many curious people, starting with cave painters and then heading to the first scientists in Ancient Greece. From there they travelled on to visit Islamic scholars and medieval monks, then narrowly avoided the Black Death that temporarily put science on pause. They journeyed on to the sixteenth century to see Copernicus, the first thinker in modern times to suggest the earth went around the sun. Next stop was in the seventeenth century to meet the stargazers Kepler and Galileo.

Have you been keeping up?

Things were only just getting going for science at this point because then they hopped over to London to visit the Royal Society men Boyle, Hooke, and Newton. After another plague and the Great Fire, they ended up at the end of the eighteenth century in the observatory of William and Caroline Herschel, a brother-and-sister team of astronomers. They declared that the scientific revolution was well and truly underway.

So where are they going now? They are teaming up with the inquisitive people of the nineteenth century and heading out on Victorian voyages of discovery. One of the big questions they are asking is "where did we come from?" – which takes them into the fascinating story of evolution.

Evolution is the process by which living things develop and change over time from earlier forms.

But they have to be careful: this is the era of Harriet's birth so they had better not meet her past self or they'll risk the implosion of space–time as we know it! The stakes have never been higher – and science has never been more curious.

Our Time Travelling Guides

Meet our guides to the ultimate questions.

Harriet is a tortoise. She was collected by Charles Darwin on his famous voyage on *The Beagle* (1831–36), which was when he explored the world and saw many things that led him to the theory of evolution. Harriet was brought back in his suitcase to England to be the family pet. As a tortoise she can live for a very long time and is well over a hundred.

Harriet

Milton is a cat. He belongs to the famous twentieth-century physicist, Erwin Schrödinger, and inspired some of his owner's best ideas. Milton is not very good at making up his mind.

Milton

Curious Quest

Having noticed some curious words over the entrance to a famous laboratory in Cambridge University, Harriet and Milton decided to go on a quest to find out the answers to as many ultimate questions as they can. In fact, they agreed to travel in time to see all the important events in the history of science.

In this series, you are invited to go with them. But look out for the Curiosity Bug hidden in some intriguing places. See how many of these you can count. Answer on page 123.

Where next for our two travellers? Down a coal mine, of course!

The Curiosity Bug

Full Steam Ahead to the Industrial Revolution!

The time machine comes to a stop and Milton nudges open the door.

"Harriet, I think we must've taken a wrong turn near Jupiter." They had made a little detour after the Herschels' observatory to take a closer look at the moons Galileo had first spotted.

"Why do you say that?" asks Harriet as she checks the fuel gauge and puts on the parking brake.

"You said we were going on an exotic cruise with your old master, Charles Darwin."

"Yes, eventually we will."

Milton's ears lie flat against his head in dismay. "But outside the box it's dark, noisy, and very hot. I don't like it. We must have landed on an alien planet!"

"Is that the only explanation you can think up?" asks Harriet.

Milton steps gingerly outside – then leaps back into the box when a pony trots by hauling a wagonload of coal. A ragged boy holds the bridle and encourages the creature along a little railway track by holding the mangled end of a carrot in front of him.

"I know where we are! We're down a coal mine!" squeaks Milton. "Why have you brought me here?"

Harriet pulls on a special dust jacket to protect her shell. "To show you the next stage in our exploration of human curiosity, of course. That was what we agreed."

"What? Deep underground? Look out there, Harriet: there are

children and animals working in the pits of the earth when they should be outside enjoying fresh air and going to school! Human curiosity has taken a very bad turn!"

"Unfortunately, that's part of the story of science. Welcome, Milton, to the Industrial Revolution." Harriet places the time machine on standby and heads for the door. "Watch your tail."

"Why don't I get a dust jacket?" asks Milton as they head out into the mine.

"Because you can reach to clean yourself with your tongue."

Milton checks his coat. Already his white patches are turning grey. "I'm not grooming that off with my tongue! Harriet, it's filthy down here."

"Well, it is a coal mine, Milton. What did you expect? Marble floors?"

Milton huffs and grumbles behind her back. "Whatever is coal made of to be so messy?"

HOW COAL IS MADE

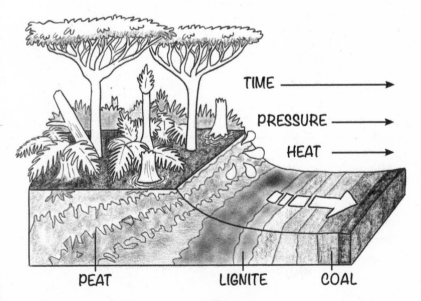

PEAT   LIGNITE   COAL

"I wondered that myself and looked it up. I could hardly believe the answer! Can you imagine that this black coal was once growing plants and trees? When these died, and if the conditions were right, they turned very slowly into rock over millions of years. That's why coal is what is called a fossil fuel." They've passed beyond the light of the time machine now so Harriet turns on her head torch, catching the shiny walls of the mine in its glare. "Put the same material under even higher pressure and you might get diamonds!"

Teacher's been under a lot of pressure recently.

Milton doesn't think that there are any precious stones down here. "I've heard that it's bad to burn coal."

"That's because burning it releases greenhouse gases. Think of all that carbon dioxide (CO_2) that had been locked away in the ancient trees over millennia, thanks to the way plants make their energy to grow by photosynthesis.

"When we use coal and other fossil fuels, we release CO_2 more quickly than it can be absorbed because we are doing in minutes what it has taken the plants millennia to capture. More CO_2 in the atmosphere results in global warming."

"Uh-oh." Milton licks his paws and grimaces. As he had feared, coal tastes horrid.

"We'll explore climate change on our next adventure. But back at this time, in around 1816, no one can see that in the future. To them, coal is a brilliant way of producing energy. Fossil fuel is about to give humanity a big push forward and leads to our own times. They would say in the nineteenth century that it is a very good thing to have coal."

"Where are we exactly?" asks Milton. He doesn't like the way the darkness is full of breezes. They ruffle his fur the wrong way. He hadn't imagined that it would be so windy underground! Very soon he is sneezing, thanks to the dust in the air.

"We are in the north of England near a town called Gateshead. This is just one of many mines in the area. They are still working it even though there was a terrible accident here a few years ago. Digging coal is extremely dangerous."

"You're not making me feel any better!" says Milton. "Why do people work down here, then?"

"Because they have to earn a living, Milton. Not everyone can live the life of a pampered pet!"

"I'm not pampered," complains Milton, but thinking that he probably is. When he eventually gets home, all he has to worry about is where to go to sleep and how to miaow so that his owner will remember to feed him.

"Their job is digging out the coal, which at this time is done mainly by hand with pickaxe and shovel. The coal is then carried up to the surface in the pony wagons, transported on to cities and factories by canals and ships, and then used in heating or to power steam engines."

"Now you're talking! Choo-choo!" says Milton. He is hoping he can persuade Harriet to take him on a train ride in this era.

"Yes, most people think of trains when I say that," agrees Harriet, "but in fact the first industrial use of a steam engine was to pump out water from a mine. Undergound tunnels often get flooded by water in the ground. Trains come a little later in this adventure."

"Who came up with the steam engine?" asks Milton, squeezing through a flap door held open by a little girl. "Thank you!"

The little girl looks so miserable that Milton leaves her an apple. It looks suspiciously like the one that fell on Newton's head in their last adventure.

"The inventor was called Thomas Newcomen – and he did that back in 1712. Around sixty years later, James Watt, another great inventor who really understood how to apply his science, came up with an engine that made a rotary motion, like you see powering the wheels of steam trains. Steam engines are the top technology during the nineteenth century – that's until the electric motor and petrol engine begin to take over. Ah, here it is!"

How does a steam train work?

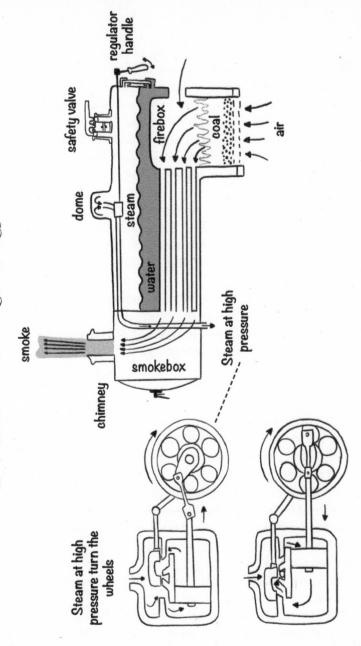

Harriet brings Milton to the pump plunger, the name given to a long pipe. The end they can see is dipped in a pool of water, sucking up the liquid like a huge straw for a giant.

"This pipe runs all the way to the surface, where the steam engine is working to pump the water out. If the engine fails, then the water down here would rapidly rise and we'd be in big trouble."

Milton decides he will very quickly learn this lesson in mining from Harriet so he can get away before the pump develops technical difficulties!

"Great – yes, I see. Very interesting. Let's go."

"That's not why we've come. We've got another historic first to investigate. Watch those men over there." Harriet nudges Milton and points to three men standing around a lamp, which they are inspecting closely.

"There's firedamp down that passageway, sir," says one miner. "We had to evacuate last week."

"What's 'firedamp'?" whispers Milton to Harriet.

"It's the term given to flammable gases," she replies.

"You mean...?"

"Yes: one spark and BOOM!"

Milton's whiskers droop. "Harriet, I want to go home."

"It will be too dangerous to send one of you to test the lantern," says the man in charge, mopping his brow with a once-white handkerchief. He looks around him for inspiration. "I know – let's send that cat!"

"What cat?" asks the miner in surprise.

"Oh – I thought you must know about it, seeing how it's sitting near your lunch box. Though I must admit, I thought it very odd that your team would bring one down here. Canaries in a mine, yes, but not cats."

"Not my cat, sir," says the miner. "Never seen him in my life before."

"Never mind, he's here and he'll do for our purposes. Here, Puss, a fish if you pull this lantern down there." The man in charge moves quickly and grabs poor Milton by the scruff of the neck.

Milton hisses but the man is too strong. The visiting scientist fashions a little string harness to go around Milton's neck.

"We need something to put the lantern on now – something flat," says the man.

Harriet is hopping from leg to leg in distress.

"Stay out of sight!" calls Milton, thinking her shell would make a suitably flat surface and then both of them would be in trouble.

"Oh, Milton, I'm so sorry. It'll be all right!" calls Harriet, keeping in the shadows. "At least I think so!"

"How about this, sir?" One of the miners presents the visitor with a little trolley used for pushing tools along.

"Perfect!" The man fastens the lit lantern on the trolley and ties it down. "Right: let's see if the design works outside the laboratory. Take cover, friends."

The visitor and the miners clearly aren't that worried about cat rights because when Milton hesitates, one bumps him on the bottom with a boot. "Hurry up, cat!"

"You'll be perfectly safe. We've tested this in our laboratory in London," says the man with confidence.

"And if you don't do it, you'll be sorry!" threatens the miner.

There's no way out of this experiment. Thinking of fish to distract himself, Milton ventures down the passageway with the cart rattling behind him. The three men stay back, crouched behind a rock. Milton does notice that the air smells foul but nothing else happens. The lamp continues to burn steadily.

"Excellent!" cries the visitor, running forward and scooping up Milton, cart, and lamp. "You clever cat! I will report to Mr Davy that his invention works!"

"What would've happened if it hadn't?" Milton asks Harriet after he receives his prize of a fish from the miner's lunch box.

"We would've been blown up in the explosion of gases," says Harriet. "That's what used to happen a lot to miners. Mr Davy, the person the visitor mentioned, is a famous man at this time, a real celebrity scientist. His full name is Sir Humphry Davy and he is asked if he can come up with a scientific solution to the problem of mine explosions. He and his talented assistant, Michael Faraday, design a lamp that encloses the flame in a wick, allowing gas through to power the flame. The crucial development is that the mesh is just the right kind – not too gappy – to stop the flame flaring back out to light up other dangerous gases in the air."

"So I wasn't in danger?"

"You weren't in danger if they got the holes the right size this time..."

Milton flops down, feeling faint. "The things I do for science!"

"I don't think they should've made you do it, but wasn't it worth seeing though? It's one of the first examples of scientific thinking being applied to industrial technology with the aim of saving lives."

"You mean it is the beginning of what now we call health and safety?" asks Milton.

"Exactly, though most places of work at this time would fail a modern inspection."

FACTORY RULES

1. CHILDREN CAN START WORK AS SOON AS THEY ARE USEFUL (AROUND 5 YEARS OLD).

2. THEY CAN WORK ALL DAY WITH NO FIXED HOURS.

3. CHIMNEY SWEEPS MAY GO UP CHIMNEYS WITHOUT PROTECTION.

4. CHILD WORKERS CAN CRAWL UNDER MACHINES WHILE THE MACHINES ARE RUNNING TO FIX PROBLEMS.

5. FRESH AIR AND REST? THAT IS ONLY ALLOWED ON SUNDAY.

AND, REMEMBER, THE MANAGEMENT TAKES ABSOLUTELY NO RESPONSIBILITY FOR ACCIDENTS OR INJURIES. WORK AT YOUR OWN RISK!

"The good news is that, throughout the nineteenth century, most countries with big industries like coal mining start to pass laws putting limits on, then stopping, the worse kind of child labour. Ready for our next stop?" asks Harriet.

Milton is very happy to escape the mine without having to wait for the law to change. "I need a bath first – then a stop."

They head back to the time machine. "All right, then. I'm going to prepare a timeline for biological advances for you while you wash. Make sure you don't use up all the hot water!" warns Harriet. "Even with this dust jacket, I'll need lots of bubble bath to get my shell back to how it was."

While Harriet and Milton clean up, let's meet the man who thought up the safety lamp.

HUMPHRY DAVY

- Lived: 1778–1829
- Number of jobs: 3 (chemist, inventor, travel writer)
- Influence (out of 100): 65 (in his own day he was immensely influential in the popularizing of science for a mass audience through his public talks at the Royal Institution, as well as for his work to isolate new chemical elements with electricity. He also gave the great scientist Michael Faraday his first laboratory job)
- Right? (out of 20): 18 (he invented what is now known as electrochemistry and turned scientific theory to practical uses with his lamp, as well as making many other fascinating discoveries)
- Helpfully wrong? (out of 10): 4 (he had an interesting failure with copper-bottomed ships. Copper sheeting protected the Royal Navy's wooden hulls but it was prone to corrosion. His solution succeeded in preserving the copper but the chemical side effect proved the perfect host for weeds and barnacles, making the ships bottom-heavy!)
- Interesting fact: he showed he had a funny side with his fondness for laughing gas (nitrous oxide). More seriously, he suggested correctly that it could be used as an anaesthetic during operations.

Science can be a funny business!

Ha Ha Ha

Harriet's Timeline of Top 19th-Century Discoveries: Part 1

Biology and medicine

1802 Jean-Baptiste Lamarck publishes theory on animal evolution through inherited characteristics

1833 William Whewell coins term "scientist" as the age sees the rise of the professional, specialized scientist

1842 As palaeontology makes great strides, Richard Owen coins term "dinosaur"

1854 Florence Nightingale heads team of nurses during Crimean War, leading to reform of nursing practices

1855 Health reformer John Snow identifies cause of cholera outbreak in London, leading to major hygiene reform

1858 Charles Darwin (and Alfred Russel Wallace) publish papers on evolution through natural selection

1859 *On the Origin of Species* published, giving Darwin's theory at greater length

1860–64 Louis Pasteur runs experiments and comes up with germ theory

1865 Gregor Mendel develops his laws of inheritance

1892 Dmitri Ivanovsky discovers viruses

How Old is the Earth? Fossil Hunting and Geologists

"Oh, Harriet, this is much better!" exclaims the newly washed Milton as he exits the time machine onto a beach. "Where and when have you brought me?"

It's a cold but clear winter's day. A stony beach runs up to the foot of a line of cliffs that have distinct horizontal lines across their face from the many different layers of rock. In the distance is a small fishing village protected by the curve of a big sea wall.

"That little port is Lyme Regis in Dorset," says Harriet. "The ancient wall is called the Cobb and has been there since medieval times. We are in 1811 and at this era it is a popular place for the rich and famous to come and bathe in the refreshing waters of the Channel."

Milton reasons that what's good for the rich must be good for him so he goes and dips a paw in a wave. He lets out a yowl. "Refreshing! You mean freezing!"

Harriet laughs. She has wisely kept dry. "Nineteenth-century doctors think the colder the better! This isn't the worst of their medical ideas, because at least their patients get to rest in the fresh air out of the coal smoke of the cities. It is safer than the bloodletting and most of the medicines they recommend."

Deciding he could still have fun without going in, Milton is getting in the holiday mood. He prances along the strand, dodging waves but only occasionally getting his paws wet.

"Milton, we did come here for a purpose!" calls Harriet.

"Which is?" The sun has come out. Milton turns around three times, scratches away some annoying seaweed, and sits down on a flat-topped rock.

Harriet painstakingly climbs up to join him. "All that digging for coal and other minerals to power the Industrial Revolution keeps throwing up strange traces of creatures buried in the rock."

Milton remembers this from his first adventure with Harriet. "I know this! You mean fossils!"[1]

"You are looking at one of the best places to find them." Harriet points to the cliffs. "That rock is called Blue Lias – which is probably just how the locals say 'blue layers'. It is deposit upon deposit of limestone and shale, formed between 195 and 200 million years ago."

Milton scrunches up his brow to remember Harriet's timeline from the very first adventure. "That's… that's the age of the dinosaurs!"

"Exactly – though those creatures haven't been named yet. I've brought you to meet the best fossil hunter of this period. Drum roll please!"

Milton obliges, stamping his paws on the flat rock. "Where is he?"

"There she is now!" Harriet points at a girl of about twelve who is carefully examining the cliffs, picking up rocks, and occasionally splitting them apart with a little hammer.

"Marvellous! So does she become a university professor and go on expeditions when she's older?" guesses Milton.

"Oh no. Mary Anning is very poor and, like all women of her day, doesn't have the chance to go to university, or in her case even to school as she has to earn a living. Her father introduced her to fossil hunting as a way of making money out of their hobby of collecting the interesting objects coming out of these cliffs. They can sell the best specimens to gentlemen scholars and less important ones to tourists."

---

1 For how fossils are made, join Harriet and Milton in *Cave Discovery*!

Milton watches Mary striding across the stones, head bent to the ground. "Sounds hard work."

"It is. When her father died last year, Mary and her older brother, Joseph, aided by their mother, Molly, were left to carry on the business. They were in serious danger of going hungry. That's her brother over there – the older boy also looking for fossils. It is Mary, however, who is to become over the next few decades the most expert collector of them all. She is able to extract whole specimens, thanks to her research and deep understanding of how the local rock reacts. She also does everything she can to educate herself about her subject; for example, dissecting animals around today who seem to be most like the fossils she is finding. That helps her discover the links between extinct animals and their modern descendants. Everyone starts coming to her for advice and even though she isn't allowed into the scientific clubs run by men, they all acknowledge her as a truly remarkable person responsible for the best finds."

Milton is quite taken with the idea of this dark-haired girl with her plain clothes and a determined expression managing to bash some sense into the brains of the learned men of this time just by being so very good at what she did. "Shall we come back and visit her when she starts making her discoveries?"

Harriet gives a secret little smile. "No need: she and her brother are about to make the first of the big finds this very day!"

Harriet has parked the time machine very near the spot of the great discovery so all they have to do is wait among the rocks for Mary and Joseph to approach. Mary has a keen eye and spots them.

"Good day, strange creature. What are you doing here?" She picks up Harriet and examines her under-shell in a manner that makes Harriet blush. "You're no native to England. I think you must've washed ashore from a wreck – which makes your friend here the ship's cat." She passes Harriet to Joseph for him to admire and strokes Milton. "Never fear, if you've lost your owners we can find you a saucer of milk and something to eat at our house. Just wait until we've finished for the day."

"She's very generous," whispers Harriet as Mary and Joseph go back to hunting. "She remains through her life a deeply committed Christian so always tries to help those less fortunate than herself. She is also free with her knowledge, letting people come with her to see how she works without charging them anything, which is amazing when you think how poor she is."

"Mary, look what that cat is sitting on," says Joseph, pushing Milton gently aside.

"My goodness!" Mary claps her hands. "What were you hiding, Mr Cat? You clever creature: you cleared away the seaweed!" She crouches down. "It's a new fossil. Look, Joseph: it's got a long skull and a saucer-like eye socket. What would you say, Joseph: four feet?"[2]

"At least. Can you see the rest of it, Mary?"

The two Anning children examine the cliff overhead.

---

2 1.22 metres.

"I think we might have to wait for the next storm to reveal it. Another little rock fall like the one last night and we'll probably see it," says Mary. "Let's work out how to get this skull home."

Harriet and Milton leave the children to their work and return to the time machine.

"Do they find the rest of it?" asks Milton, putting a little shell fossil Mary gave him in his box of treasures.

"Oh yes. Mary finds it nine metres up the cliff. The creature, which comes to be called an ichthyosaur, is in total over five metres long."

SAFETY NOTICE!

Fossil collecting can be very dangerous due to the unstable rock in which fossils are usually found. Mary was very skilled at what she did but even she almost died in 1833 in a rockslide that killed her beloved dog, Tray. Never go fossil hunting on a beach or quarry without first checking with an expert where it is safe to go!

"I thought it looked a bit like a swordfish," says Milton, licking his lips.

"It certainly was once a huge marine creature. The name means 'fish lizard' in Greek, but it is in fact a reptile, not a fish. Mary is one of the people who found the evidence that the world is very much older than people had thought and that there were traces of huge numbers of extinct creatures to be found in the rock. You probably know many of these as dinosaurs, but there are others: sea creatures, shells, more recent fossils of big mammals like the mammoth."

Dinosaur means "terrible lizard", a term made up by Richard Owen in 1842 to describe the huge fossil creatures.

How do you best raise an Argentinosaurus baby? With a crane![3]

"Mary made five major discoveries," continues Harriet, "and hundreds of other smaller ones. She helped change our big picture of just how long it took the world to become what we see today. Unfortunately, the gentlemen scholars often took credit for what were really her discoveries as they got to announce them in their clubs and societies."

---

3 *Argentinosaurus huinculensis* is thought to be the biggest land creature ever!

Mary's Big Five

1. The ichthyosaur

2. First complete *Plesiosaurus*

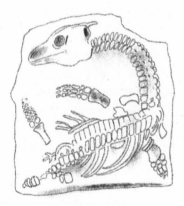

3. First British example of a pterosaur – called a flying dragon when put on display by the British Museum!

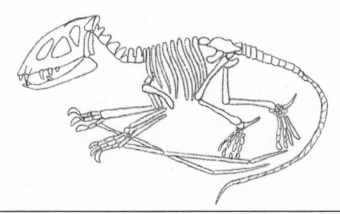

4. *Squaloraja*, a new fossil fish

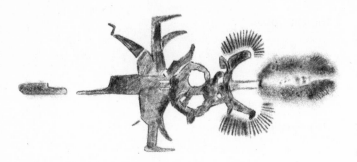

5. A wonderful Plesiosaurus in a curled-up position, called "the most beautiful" specimen of its kind

Other curious finds include...

6. She was among the first to suggest that the strange conical objects known as "bezoar" stones were in fact dinosaur poo!

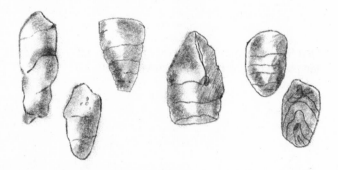

7. She noticed that the *sepia* (a fossil cuttlefish) specimen still had its fossilized ink sack. She ground this up and turned it back into ink and used it to make drawings of the specimens! Creatures of the age of dinosaurs drawn in Jurassic ink!

JUST HOW OLD IS THE EARTH?

It was very hard for people in Mary's time to work out how old the earth really is, as they were only just discovering that it was much older than they had thought! They also had limited tools to date things. What had they consulted before this time? They had used one of the oldest objects they knew – the Bible – added together all the dates that they could find in the Old Testament (the part that starts with Adam and Eve), and came up with a figure that suggested the earth was indeed old – but only a few thousand years old.

The world was created precisely at 6 p.m. on Saturday 22 October 4004 BC.

Not all Christians, of course, treated the Bible as if it was a science text book. They chose to look instead at the evidence they could see around them. One of these people was James Hutton, a Scottish gentleman farmer, who in 1795 published a book called *Theory of the Earth*, which suggested that we date the earth from what we see happening in front of our eyes. His theory suggested that the covering of the earth is continually recycled and he thought it might be the result of immense pressure and heat from underneath throwing up seabeds (which is why you can find fossil sea creatures up mountains!) and then eroding down again to become ocean bottoms once more.

He found some key evidence to support this when he searched for, and discovered, a spot at the junction of two mountain ranges. He saw that granite – a very hard stone – had penetrated deep into the schists (crystalline rocks) and limestones. That proved that granite must have once been hot molten rock forced in under pressure.

This was a good day for science, but a bad day for those who wanted to count the age of the earth by using Bible stories, which had never been written with that purpose in the first place!

There were two challenges here for the traditional big picture of where we come from. Until then, people had assumed the surface of the earth was the result of what was left over after Noah's flood. The second was that for Hutton's idea to work, you need a long time.

A really really long time!

Not thousands but millions of years.

Not all the scientists agreed with Hutton. Here are the main alternatives:

Neptunists – led by the German expert Abraham Werner – who thought that the world is formed from four types of actions by water and that the oldest rock rose out of a universal ocean.

Genesis-based account – led by Jean-André de Luc, who reasoned that the account of the seven days of creation could be read as six epochs ending with the Flood. Each makes a very long day.

Vulcanists – unsurprisingly they thought the earth was a result of volcanic action!

Catastrophists – led by the influential Georges Cuvier, often called the founder of palaeontology. They thought the surface of the earth was the result of a series of catastrophes, or big upsets.

Uniformitarians – led by James Hutton, who said the earth experienced slow change over immense periods of time. He had a famous follower called Charles Lyell, whose book, *Principles of Geology* (1830–33), was one of the works Darwin took with him on his voyage on *The Beagle*. It was this view that came to be accepted by the majority by the middle of the nineteenth century, in part thanks to Mary's fossils!

And the answer to how old the earth is? Guess![4]

Palaeontology is the study of fossil plants and animals.

---

4 Answer: 4.54 billion years ± 0.05 billion years!

WILLIAM BUCKLAND

The Victorian world of fossil hunting and geology is stuffed full of layer upon layer of wonderfully eccentric characters! We only have time to dig up one. Arguably the most outrageous among them was the first ever Professor of Geology at Oxford University and friend of Mary Anning, Reverend William Buckland. It was he who made the public announcements of her big finds. (We met him in *Cave Discovery* making a mistake over the Red Lady of Paviland!)

- Lived: 1784–1856
- Number of jobs: 2 (theologian and geologist)
- Influence (out of 100): 48 (not the most important figure in geology, but had some good ideas)
- Right? (out of 20): 12 (he said that you shouldn't look to the Bible for scientific truth, and that helped many who were struggling to change their big picture of how the earth was created)
- Helpfully wrong? (out of 10): 4 (he started by believing he'd found evidence of the biblical flood but had the good scientific approach of changing his mind when he saw that the glaciation theory of the Swiss Louis Agassiz was a better explanation)
- Interesting fact: there are so many wonderful facts about him; here are just a few. His house in Oxford was full of specimens, fossil and living ones, including at one point a jackal and five guinea pigs. After dinner it was noticed that the jackal had also dined and there was only one guinea pig left! His children were allowed to ride their pony inside the house and he had a pet bear called Tiglath Pileser who came dressed as a student to many university functions.

GALAPAGOS NEAR MISS!
DARWIN AND 'THE BEAGLE'

"Now we've settled the age of the earth," declares Harriet, "I think you're ready to meet my master, Charles Darwin. He is starting his voyage to discover where humans and all creatures come from."

Milton has been giving this some thought. "Harriet, what would happen if we met you?"

"What do you mean?"

"Well, isn't this around the time you were born? If you meet you, then what will the universe do?"

Harriet pauses, her claw over the "Go" button on the dashboard. "That is an excellent question, Milton, and one I should've considered more seriously. The answer is that I don't know. Our bodies change all the time as cells are replaced but we do keep some permanent structures, like cartilage and enamel in our teeth, all our life."

"So the Harriet of this time has some of the same matter as you do?"

"Yes."

"That is a paradox: to have the same matter in two places at once!" Milton is very proud of this word.

> A paradox is a situation that is impossible or hard to understand because it contains two opposing or contradictory facts.

"It certainly is. Time travel is full of them. I think, though, for the sake of the space–time continuum I'd better avoid meeting myself. The universe might just shrug it off – or it might explode. I'll need you to keep an eye out for a younger me and make sure we stay apart!"

"I'll make sure I keep alert at all times," promises Milton. "Where are we catching up with Darwin?"

"Another good question!" says Harriet. "My master set sail in late December 1831 on board a survey ship called HMS *Beagle*. His job was to be the ship's naturalist. He was only twenty-two but ready for an adventure. He'd already shown that he loved collecting things. When he was a student at Cambridge, he liked nothing better than to collect insects. He would always pick up interesting beetles, but when he ran out of hands for a third specimen, he'd pop it in his mouth!"

"Poor beetle!" shudders Milton.

DARWIN'S UNUSUAL BEETLE-COLLECTING METHOD*

*Do not try this at home!

"Big ideas like Darwin's don't come out of nowhere. You should know that he had an excellent book list for the sea journey."

"I imagine he had a lot of time for reading," says Milton.

"Yes, the voyage lasted five years. His cabin doubled as the ship's library so he didn't even have to get out of bed to fetch a book! Looking at what he read helps explain where his theory came from."

"You mean like the list of ingredients for a recipe with the added genius of the chef to produce the final result!" suggests Milton.

"Exactly," agrees Harriet. "Here are a few of the things he read."

TOP PICKS FROM DARWIN'S *BEAGLE* BOOKSHELF

- Charles Lyell's *Principles of Geology* – Darwin needed to know that the earth changed slowly over time for his theory.
- Alexander von Humboldt's *Personal Narrative* – in the nineteenth century this fascinating German was the world's most famous naturalist. He had the most places and things named after him, and established the idea of what we now call an ecosystem, or how nature is interlinked. He was also the first to spot human-made climate change.

- Jean-Baptiste Lamarck's *Natural History of Invertebrate Animals* – this French naturalist suggested animals adapted to their environment, by use or disuse of certain characteristics, and that these changes could be inherited by their offspring, sometimes called "soft inheritance" evolution.

- Georges Cuvier's *The Animal Kingdom* – this French thinker, last seen debating the age of the earth, founded palaeontology and established extinction as a fact – a vital idea in Darwin's theory.
- John Herschel's *The Preliminary Discourse on the Study of Natural Philosophy*[5] – this was the first general scientific method published since Francis Bacon's (whom we met in Shakespeare's Globe Theatre). Remember John Herschel – because he is going to come in later!
- John Milton's *Paradise Lost* – a famous poem about Adam and Eve and the Garden of Eden.
- Samuel Richardson's *The History of Sir Charles Grandison* – a love story; the days at sea were very long but then so is the book!
- And lots of travel stories – what else!

"So Darwin is swinging in his hammock, reading away…" muses Milton.

"He's doing much more than that: he's collecting, thinking, exploring…"

"Yes, yes, you interrupted me! I was having a great thought."

---

5 The name for "science" at the time.

"Sorry, Milton." Harriet waves at him to continue.

"So he knows that geologists have found proof that the earth's surface changes slowly over long periods of time?"

"Yes."

"And he knows from fossil hunters like Mary Anning that animals have gone extinct?"

"Yes. And he sees it for himself when he visits a fossil site in Argentina called Punta Alta. He observes traces of huge land mammals long gone, but who appear to have smaller similar versions still living, like the armadillo."

"So he gets the idea from Lamarck, Cuvier, and others that perhaps animals might change over time too?"

"Correct."

"But this process is difficult to see because it happens so slowly?"

"Indeed. Difficult to see until he reaches the Galapagos – which is exactly where we are landing. I'll need you to be on High Harriet Alert!"

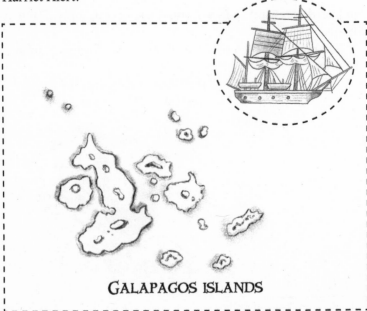

GALAPAGOS ISLANDS

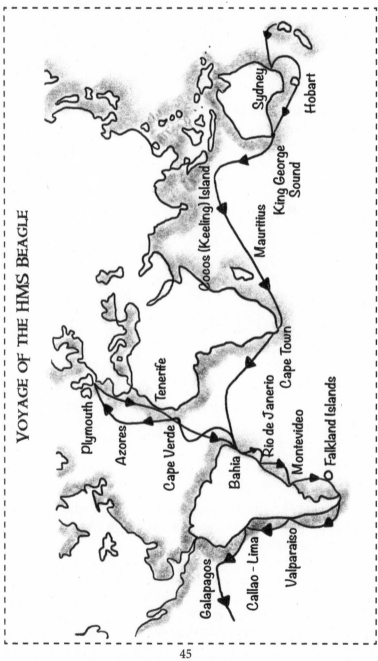

VOYAGE OF THE HMS BEAGLE

Plymouth
Azores
Tenerife
Cape Verde
Bahia
Rio de Janerio
Montevideo
Falkland Islands
Galapagos
Callao – Lima
Valparaiso
Cape Town
Cocos (Keeling) Island
Mauritius
King George Sound
Sydney
Hobart

The two time travellers get out of the box and find themselves right at Charles Darwin's feet. Fortunately, it is rough volcanic terrain and he is surrounded by his nets and collection boxes so he doesn't notice them. What is worse, though, than almost being trodden on by Darwin is that they are in the middle of a whole islandful of tortoises! How on earth is Milton going to spot Young Harriet among all these?

Darwin is talking to his assistant, a cabin boy, who is already loaded down with lots of cages and nets. To be honest, the boy is looking a little glum.

"I'm guessing he's wondering about lunchtime," whispers Milton. "I bet his master doesn't think much about eating when he gets excited about science – rather like a tortoise I know who grew up in Darwin's household!"

"I do care about lunch," says Harriet. "In fact, just over there is a lovely cactus. I haven't had a mouthful of that since I was little." She starts to plod off in the direction of her snack.

"Harriet, come back!" hisses Milton. "What if you meet you?"

But Harriet is soon lost in the field of tortoises and he can no longer see her.

"Oh my whiskers, what am I to do? The universe may come to an end just because Harriet got hungry! I always thought I was the one likely to upset things because of my appetite, not her."

Before Harriet can get a bite of her cactus, someone else steps in. Darwin scoops Harriet from the ground.

"Look here, Eddie. Do you see that this tortoise is different from all the others? She looks just like the one I collected from James Island. Do you remember?"

"Yes, sir. Those tortoises were rounder, blacker, and much tastier than these ones on Hood Island!" agrees the boy.

Oh no, things have suddenly got much, much worse! Milton has been worrying that Harriet was going to bump into herself at the cactus and risk ending the universe; now the cabin boy seems hungry enough to eat her!

"I say, she does look very like my specimen – in fact, identical! Look at the shell markings." Darwin gets out a notebook and compares Harriet to a sketch he had made. "Either she stowed away in my bag or I have found two matching tortoises – remarkable! Let's take her back to the ship."

Let's not, thinks Milton. But how can he stop the two humans from taking Harriet back to *The Beagle* and imploding time? He scampers in pursuit, taking shelter behind every rock and stone whenever he's in danger of being spotted.

"Intriguing, isn't it, Eddie, how the tortoises are so different on each island from the other species just a few miles away?" says Darwin.

"Yes, sir. Do you think they've got tortoise soup for lunch again?"

"Very likely – best source of fresh meat in these parts."

"It's a little like what you were saying about your finches, Mr

Darwin," adds Eddie, showing he does have other, non-food related thoughts. "How the beaks in the different species vary greatly even though these are just a tiny group of isolated islands."

Darwin pats Eddie on the back, almost making him drop his burdens. "Indeed, one might fancy that with few birds here, one species of finch has been taken and modified for different ends. From what I see, each beak excels at a certain feeding task. What a marvellous place! I'm astonished at the amount of creative force that is displayed on these small, barren, rocky islands!"

SPOT THE DIFFERENCE!

They get on board the ship's boat. Fortunately Eddie has gathered up the time machine, not noticing it among the many packages he is already carrying. Milton slips aboard and sneaks inside the box once the oarsmen get underway. He's had an idea.

"Hello, Time Machine. We're in a bit of a fix!" he says.

```
      I can see that. You are about to
         destroy the universe - maybe.
```

"We'll be fine as long as I can keep the Harriets apart. Please can you locate her for me?"

```
She's right outside in Darwin's pocket.
```

"Not that one – the other one!"

The time machine whirrs and blips for ten seconds before coming back with a message.

```
         I need input from my readers.
```

Where have Harriet and Harriet got to? Can you spot them as they ramble around the ship and help Milton stop them meeting?

51

I have finally caught up with the other
Harriet. She is currently by Darwin's
bookshelf.

"That's her! So all I have to do is stop Darwin reaching his cabin before Older Harriet has a chance to escape?"

Or you could run ahead and persuade
Younger Harriet to hide.

Milton sees at once that this is a better idea, as Darwin shows no sign of letting his new tortoise escape before he's had a chance to compare them. Our brave time traveller, however, has the advantage of four legs. As soon as the boat bumps against the side of the ship, he scrambles up a rope and through the legs of the sailors waiting to receive the latest delivery of specimens.

"Oi! Where did that cat come from?" yells one sailor.

Milton doesn't wait for an answer but evades all attempts to catch him. He's not sure exactly where he is going but Harriet has already told him Darwin's cabin is in the library so he is following the smell of leather.

He bursts into the cabin to find a tortoise perched on a reading desk. To an outsider it would look like she is thinking of nibbling at the book, but Milton knows, as this is Harriet, she is teaching herself to read.

"Harriet?"

"Do I know you, sir?" She is indeed very like his Harriet but perhaps a little less wrinkled. Her tone is unmistakable. She's annoyed with him interrupting her reading.

Milton dances on the spot. It's nice to know his Harriet hasn't changed much. "Yes, you will do. I'll explain later but for now, you have to hide!" He will keep his promise to explain, but not until he's back with his old Harriet – he doesn't want to mess up the timeline!

"Hide? Why would I want to do that?"

"Because… because terrible things will happen if you don't!"

"I beg to differ. Terrible things will happen if I do. Don't you know that these barbaric sailors dine on my kind every evening? I'm only safe in here under Mr Darwin's protection."

That is a hitch in the plan Milton hadn't considered. "I'll keep you safe!" he promises, rashly. "We'll have to disguise you."

He looks around for inspiration, finds an officer's hat, and puts it on the floor. "Get under that. We have to leave this very moment."

"Or else?"

"Or else the universe ends right now."

Obviously, Younger Harriet does not understand him, except that he is serious and urgent about his request. With a dignified sigh, she scuttles under the hat. "Now what?"

"Now follow me."

"I can't see."

"True. I'll push. You just keep moving."

And so the odd duo, a cat and a travelling hat, set off into *The Beagle*.

Harriet is deeply regretting her decision to snack on her favourite cactus. She doesn't know what came over her, except perhaps a longing to recapture the taste of her youth. Finally Mr Darwin lifts her out of his pocket. She closes her eyes – but the universe doesn't come to an end. Milton must have got her other self away and saved the day!

"Now let me have a closer look at you." Darwin takes measurements and weighs her. "Put on a little weight since I last checked, but, as there's only one of you here, I assume you must've smuggled yourself into my boxes and tried to make a run for it." He places her on the table in front of an open book. "Stay there, Harriet. I want to take you home with me. You are better off with me as you'd never fit in with the tortoises of Hood Island. They're a different species. What a fascinating place the Galapagos is."

He sits next to her and begins to write up his journal. Harriet looks around the cabin and spots the time machine at the bottom of a stack of specimen boxes that Eddie has left in one corner. Darwin mustn't find that. Slowly, slyly, she starts to edge towards it.

"Oh no you don't, Miss Harriet!" exclaims Darwin. But just as he is about to pick her up again, there's a knock at the door.

"Look what I found in the corridor!" says the captain. "My hat with your tortoise in it!"

"Captain FitzRoy, I do apologize." Confused, Darwin rushes to retrieve his pet.

Milton streaks into the room between the legs of the ship's commander and makes straight for the time machine. Harriet catches a brief glimpse of herself in the hand of the captain before she scuttles inside the box. Milton slams the door behind him.

"Go, go!" he yowls.

Harriet doesn't bother to input any directions but just presses the nearest button. The time machine winks out of existence in 1835. Catastrophe is narrowly avoided – this time.

TRY THIS AT HOME: BECOME A NATURALIST LIKE YOUNG DARWIN

Darwin's amazing career as a scientist began by looking at his feet – no, really! If you go outside into a garden or park, you can do the same and start your career as a biologist. All you will need is:

1. A pencil and pad

2. Somewhere to go – preferably a wild spot, but a garden, school field, or park will do. Make sure you ask permission and take an adult with you.

3. And if you want to be super-scientific, you can use a quadrat.[6] This is a square of a size you can easily carry (about a metre) – it can be marked out in sticks or with string too. You can then compare what you see in your quadrat by moving it from place to place.

4. Now sit and look very closely. Can you see any insects or larger animals? How many different plants? Do you know what they are?

5. Look at the shape of the leaves, seeds, or colour of the flowers. How do the creatures you see get about? Do they fly, crawl, walk? Can you work out what they eat? Can you spot anything that makes these plants or creatures well suited to these conditions, e.g. colourful flowers to attract bees?

Then write up your journal, just as Darwin wrote up his notes from *The Beagle*. You never know: you might change science yourself if you follow in his footsteps!

---

6 For information on how to use a quadrat you can see more here: https://www.bbc.com/bitesize/guides/z83qcj6/revision/3

Under southern skies

"Scientific exploration is more dangerous than I thought!" pants Milton, sprawled on his back, paws in the air. "Never again, Harriet. I want a list of all the places where you've been so I know where we should avoid."

Harriet checks the locator screen. In her random selection, she has spun them off to the moon and they aren't ready for that adventure yet. She sets a new time and place.

"Fortunately for our next stop with Mr Darwin, I remember that I was kept inside with a bad cold and never landed at this spot."

"And where is that?"

"Cape Town in South Africa. My master is about to meet one of his personal heroes: Sir John Herschel. It is his book I pointed out in *The Beagle*'s library."

"Any relation of our friends William and Caroline, the astronomer brother and sister from our last adventure?"

"John is William's son and another stargazer. He's moved his family to Cape Town to make the first astronomical survey of the southern hemisphere."

"Oh, are the stars different in the south then?"

"Yes! The north pole faces out into the universe beyond, whereas the south faces into the Milky Way, our galactic centre. Go south and you are looking out into a field of bright stars, including constellations like the one that contains the Southern Cross. Herschel is charting them so they become as well known as the familiar ones in the north.

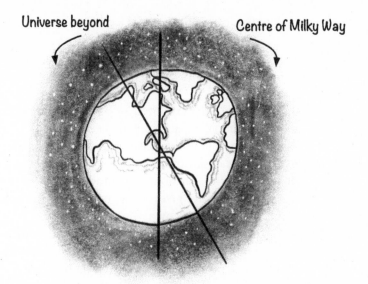

Universe beyond

Centre of Milky Way

"He also has another purpose: he wants to take new measurements on some double stars tracked by his father that are visible in the south. This is so he can test whether Newton's gravity laws work the same in distant parts of the universe. He wants to check that the big picture of the universe obeying laws – the one that Newton came up with – is for all places, not just earth."

"How can he find that out by looking at double stars?"

"It's an excellent piece of scientific reasoning. Telescopes can't see planets in other solar systems at this time so the best thing to look at is binary, or double, stars. His father thought that the two suns orbited around a common centre, which would show gravity at work. More measurements would help prove that." Harriet checks the view through the porthole. "Right: we've arrived. It's 1836 and *The Beagle* is on her way home from her long voyage around the world."

They emerge from the box to find the two scientists admiring Herschel's telescope, which he has had specially erected in his garden at Newlands, his house in Cape Town. They've arrived in a beautiful place with a flat-topped mountain behind. The skies are breathtakingly clear. Milton and Harriet sneak under the telescope.

"You must have had a wonderful voyage, Mr Darwin," says Herschel, adjusting the lens so his guest might admire the Southern Cross.

"Indeed, the riches of the rainforest in Brazil were enough to make me shout 'Hosanna!'" The young man grins.

"You were lucky to walk in the midst of wonders. Every object that falls in our way can illustrate some principle, teach us, and impress on us a sense of harmony and order in the universe. Looking at the world always gives me a conception of a power and intelligence superior to my own."

"I've always admired your book, Sir John. We have it with us on *The Beagle*. I often find myself quoting you on the mystery of mysteries – the first appearance of new beings on this earth."

"I'm flattered you've taken that to heart, Darwin."

"Where do you think creatures come from, sir?"

"I'm with the geologists like Lyell. I don't believe the creator exhausted his combinations in one act but continues to do so in constant change. We should apply this thinking to biology."

"That is my intention, Sir John. I plan to write up my voyage and then reason through what I've learned on true Baconian principles: looking at the facts to draw out a theory, not squeezing facts to suit my views."

"Excellent. I look forward to reading your conclusions."

The two men walk to the house through the cool of the evening. Harriet and Milton emerge to have a look through the telescope lens.

"It's fascinating to see Darwin as a young man. I'm so used to the photographs of him with the big white beard," says Milton.

"That's also partly thanks to Herschel," says Harriet, getting out her notebook to jot down some observations. "He helped the pioneers of photos with a better fixer to develop their images. He also suggested to one of them, Henry Fox Talbot, that 'photography' would be a very good name for the new process."

Milton lazes on the grass while Harriet takes a measurement of a binary star. "It was interesting to hear them talk about their big picture. Both of them seemed to believe that the universe had an intelligent design, or creator, behind it."

"Herschel certainly does and continues to do so. Darwin makes changes to his big picture as the years pass. He starts off believing in God but gets increasingly more unsure there's a creator behind it all. He ends up still admiring the grandeur of the design but he is probably best called a deist or agnostic."

"What does that mean?"

"That he doesn't say either way if a creator exists. It's a big step in a religious society to say there is no God, even if he did have a settled view against. I think we need to go back to England a few years later to see where he is going with his thinking. Ready?"

Milton rolls over. "Ready for what?"

"*On the Origin of Species*, the book that shook the world."

Milton bounds over to the time machine. "Yes!"

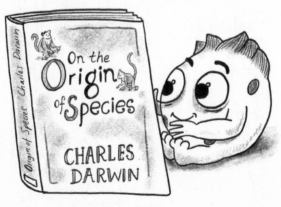

THE GREAT DEBATE! THE THEORY OF EVOLUTION

Harriet has a few minutes to set the scene now the time machine is heading happily into the future.

"My master brings me home and spends some years thinking about what he saw on his voyage. However, as you will have noticed from his bookshelf, he is not the only one to be having thoughts that might lead along the lines of a theory of evolution."

Milton checks the timeline she has given him. "So it is a race to be the first to come out with it?"

"Indeed. And it is almost a photo finish!"

"Good thing they've invented photography, then."

VICTORIAN PHOTO FINISH

"His closest rival is a naturalist called Alfred Russel Wallace, who even sends a scientific paper to him that Darwin admits is exactly the same theory he is already devising. Friends urge Darwin quickly to write up his own thoughts. He does so and the two papers – Wallace's and Darwin's – are published together by a scientific society in London in 1858. Darwin then goes one better and gives his new theory in a book with the catchy title *On the Origin of Species by Means of Natural Selection*. It is published in 1859 and causes a storm."

"Why?"

"Because people are quick to see how it changes the big picture they were used to in which mankind is described as a special creation. Some find that the idea of so many extinctions goes against their idea of a caring God."

MEET MR GLOOMY FORECAST

In the introduction to his book, Darwin called his "theory of evolution through natural selection" the doctrine, or belief, of Malthus applied to the whole animal and vegetable kingdom. This was part of what shocked his contemporaries. So who was Malthus?

Meet Mr Gloomy Forecast: Thomas Robert Malthus (1766–1834). He claimed that population always grew quicker than production, as more food equals healthy adults and that leads to more babies! This continues until there is a catastrophe of too many mouths to feed and not enough to go around, and the population collapses. Malthus shocked people because he applied his idea to humans as well as other animals. It challenged the big picture idea that many held that they were living in a friendly world that would always look after their needs.

GLOOMY GROWTH MODEL

"Most alarming for others is the idea that humans might have evolved from earlier forms," continues Harriet.

"Like the creatures we met on our first adventure, Lucy and Little Foot?"

"Yes, but those fossils haven't yet been found. Victorians are thinking more about the other apes and monkeys like the ones you can see in a zoo. And this leads us to the Great Debate in 1860, which takes place at the Oxford University Museum of Natural History." Harriet goes to the door.

"Are we quite sure we're safe?" asks Milton. "You aren't going to pop out from under someone's hat and end the universe?"

"No, we're safe. My master has become too ill with stress to come so he has sent someone to speak on his behalf." Harriet turns off the engine. "I'm looking forward to hearing what was actually said because the stories spread about this after the event have rather sensationalized the debate. I suspect the truth is less exaggerated."

The time machine has landed on a grassy patch in front of a tall, turreted building. It looks new, its stone still a honey colour and not yet blackened by smoke from coal fires. There are signs the stonemasons haven't yet finished their work decorating the doorway and windows as some of the carvings are incomplete. People are crowding up the short flight of steps and into the vast hall of the museum. It looks like a cross between a greenhouse and a railway station: cast iron pillars in tree shapes holding up a glass roof. Or maybe it is a temple to science? wonders Milton.

"Who is speaking against Darwin's theory in this debate?" he asks as they make their way to the front of the crowd.

"The main critic is a Fellow of the Royal Society and Bishop of Oxford called Samuel Wilberforce, whose father is the famous William Wilberforce who led the campaign to end slavery. There he is now, talking with Professor Acland. I think you'd like Acland: he is the man who made sure this museum was built and always takes an even-handed position. Let's go and listen in to what they are saying."

MEET THE SCIENTIST

HENRY ACLAND

Though Acland doesn't have many discoveries to his name, he was a vital link between other scientists, often taking the role of peacemaker and promoter of their work. Thanks to his persuasive powers, he reformed the way science was taught at the time.

- Lived: 1815–1900
- Number of jobs: 2 (doctor and science educator)
- Influence (out of 100): 62 (he reformed the teaching of science at Oxford University, fought opposition to get the university museum built, and became a leading health campaigner. He also sponsored the study of art and archaeology!)
- Right? (out of 20): 19 (a clean sweep! He identified the cause of cholera outbreak in Oxford as dirty water and made sure the water supply was reconstructed; he also influenced Florence Nightingale in her pursuit of better nursing practices)
- Helpfully wrong? (out of 10): 0 (for his time, seems to get most things right!)
- Interesting fact: he and his wife were both very concerned for the poor and opened their own house every Sunday as a refuge for chimney sweeps. As a doctor, he treated both rich and poor.

The two time travellers sneak past everyone to reach the men thanks to the excellent cover offered by the hooped skirts of the ladies. Professor Acland is admiring the crowds that have come to hear this important debate.

"I read your review of Mr Darwin's interesting work, Bishop Wilberforce." Acland tucks his thumbs into his waistcoat. "I thought you very fair, writing that rejecting scientific facts because they seem to be contrary to what is in the Bible is but another form of lying for God. Very well put."

"Thank you, Acland. I'm yet to be convinced, though, that Darwin has all his facts straight on this evolution-by-natural-selection matter. I will note also in the debate that he is yet to persuade all the leaders in his field. There seems to be some missing links in his arguments. I must also admit on religious grounds that I find it degrading to think that there is a such brutish origin for 'man who is created in the image of God' – very unsettling."

Acland smiles in sympathy. "New ideas always are difficult, but maybe we just need to look at them as fresh opportunities? I'm with your colleague at the university church. The Reverend Temple says we must look for the finger of God in the laws of nature themselves, even this one of evolution. Ah, here's Professor Huxley, who will speak on behalf of Mr Darwin. I believe we are ready to start."

The men shake hands and take their places at the front of the audience.

"So the bishop wants to follow the facts but doesn't like where they are leading?" whispers Milton.

"That's right. Other people, including Henry Acland and the Reverend Frederick Temple, don't have the same problem. They are quicker to adjust their big picture. Acland will go on to argue – as he tries to make peace between the warring scientific factions – that even if there is no material difference to be found between humans and apes, it wouldn't make humans the brute the bishop fears. Humans are still spiritual beings. Acland also advises the clergy not to take sides in scientific disputes – very good advice."

"You're right: I do like the sound of him!"

The crowd settles down and the debate begins. It is already getting quite heated when Huxley approaches the subject of human origins going back to apes.

The bishop leaps up. "So would you be descended from a monkey on your grandmother or your grandfather's side, sir?"

Huxley flushes with anger. "I'd prefer that than to be related to a man who uses his great gifts to obscure the truth as you are doing!"

A lady gasps at the rude insults but the two debaters both act as if they've scored debating points off each other. Both seem very pleased with themselves.

"That's the bit everyone will remember," whispers Harriet. "Not the fact that they did debate the science behind the theory. It's often forgotten that though Huxley is impressed by Darwin's amassing of facts from the *Beagle* voyage, even he isn't sure natural selection is correct. He regards it as the best picture yet to be presented until more is known, such as the mechanism by which it happens."

"Mechanism?" Milton skips behind a glass case as the crowd begins to leave. The ladies' skirts are lethal, like great bells swinging as they walk.

"How characteristics are passed from one creature to its descendants – you need this to make sense of the theory. We know now this is due to genetic inheritance but the Victorians didn't have that piece of the puzzle yet. The work of the pioneer in this field isn't yet well known."

PEAS TO MEET YOU, GREGOR MENDEL!

Working quietly away at this time in a monastery in Brno, in what is now the Czech Republic, is Gregor Mendel. Say hello to the father of genetics!

- Lived: 1822–84
- Number of jobs: 2 (scientist and friar, later abbot of St Thomas' Abbey, Brno)
- Influence (out of 100): 89 (this Austrian monk had an interest in plant inheritance, successfully identifying the rules of Mendelian inheritance through his experiments with peas. By cross-breeding different strains, he worked out that peas had dominant and recessive characteristics)
- Right? (out of 20): 16 (excellent investigative work, but not given recognition in his own day. Darwin, for example, does not appear to have read him. His work was rediscovered in the twentieth century)
- Helpfully wrong? (out of 10): 0 (he was on the right track. We'll see where this leads in our last adventure!)
- Interesting fact: he also experimented with breeding bees but that proved less popular when they stung visitors a bit too often. He was asked to get rid of what he called his "dearest little animals".

Science is easy-peasy!

"So where does that leave your master, Mr Darwin, his theory, and the new big picture?" asks Milton as they trot back to the time machine.

"The theory remains something people argue about. As the evidence from fossils and genetics mounts, though, it gains more support and it emerges as the best big picture to explain how life changes over long periods of time."

"What about how this fits with religion?"

"That depends on your approach. For some it seems to contradict the Bible, so they oppose it. Other Christians read the Bible for what it could teach them about God, not science. Acland is one of the most open-minded. He says that no one supposes that the way people currently read the Bible or understand natural science is final, showing how the big picture always changes as human wisdom grows."

"I agree," says Milton. "In our journey we've seen that the big picture always changes, sometimes with great big shifts that cause a lot of upsets."

"And those who don't believe in God take it as fitting into their big picture of a world that doesn't need a creator, like with our friend Olympe and the French materialists of the previous century."[7]

---

7 To meet the poodle Olympe, go to *Hunt with Newton!*

MONSIEUR POSITIVE – AUGUSTE COMTE

… or should we say, first modern philosopher of science! Comte's ideas influenced many famous thinkers, including Karl Marx, the founder of Communism. Comte's ideas appealed to those who favoured the idea that society evolved from one stage to another.

- Lived: 1798–1857
- Number of jobs: 1 (philosopher)
- Influence (out of 100): 71 (in his six volume *Positive Philosophy* (1830–42), this French philosopher set out his view that the only real kind of knowledge was scientific and had to be arrived at by strict scientific method. His major argument was that the human race had passed through two phases: 1) a time of belief in God or gods, and 2) a stage where people believed they were controlled by poorly understood forces. Now he thought we had entered 3) a scientific or "positive" age)

To understand a science, it is necessary to know its history.

- Right? (out of 20): ? (impossible to mark a philosophy! He uses philosophical arguments to say that only scientific knowledge can be trusted. But where does that leave his idea, because he hasn't arrived at it through scientific method? He also pays little attention to other forms of knowledge that don't, or can't, come from science)
- Helpfully wrong? (out of 10): ? (again impossible to give a mark to something that is an opinion)
- Interesting fact: Comte proposed setting up a "Religion of Humanity", as he valued the unifying role played by the church in society but didn't believe in God. This led to the setting up of secular temples in some parts of the world.

RED CLAWS AND DOVER BEACH

The new scientific ideas had a huge impact on writers of the day. A couple of their phrases are still used today when talking about Darwin and the changing big picture, so you might find them cropping up without anyone saying where they come from. Harriet wants you to know the source!

The most famous poet of the time was Alfred, Lord Tennyson, who published a long poem in 1850 grieving for a lost friend called *In Memoriam* – or "In Memory". It includes a line about the new ideas on extinction where he calls Nature "red in tooth and claw".

RED IN TOOTH
AND CLAW

This was then applied to natural selection by critics and supporters of Darwin. Tennyson also has a great verse about the new geology, describing the solid land like shifting clouds.

Another poet of the changed big picture was Matthew Arnold. His poem "Dover Beach" (1851) picks up on the idea found in Comte's work of society changing to a new post-religion phase:

The Sea of Faith... its melancholy, long, withdrawing roar

That is often used to sum up the sense that the old certainties of the old big picture were changing for some Victorians. So now when you see these phrases, you know who made them up!

"And Darwin? What does he think?" asks Milton.

"He is in two minds. I'm sorry to say he is hit hard in later life by personal tragedy and doubts. He writes to Acland about this in 1865. He says that it seems to go against common sense to look at the world and not see it originating with an express design. He then goes on to say that when he looks more closely, he doesn't believe any single structure was designed in the common meaning of the word."

"Um…" Milton is feeling quite confused.

"He means no single thing appears to be made to a fixed plan. However, Darwin does agree with Acland that assuming purpose or design in the grand scheme is one of the surest and simplest roads to discovery in natural history. For him, it is a helpful big picture, if not one he can completely believe."

"He's on the fence?"

"Yes, I think so."

Milton flicks up his tail. "As an indecisive cat, I think I'll join him."

A Brief Interlude for Codebreaking!

Milton isn't sure what he was expecting but it isn't this. Harriet's next stop on the Curious Science Quest is not another museum or laboratory but a garden in Baghdad. They haven't been back there since the Islamic Golden Age of Science.[8]

"I say, Harriet, this is splendid!" Milton puts on his sunglasses against the dazzle of the sun and admires the waterwheel in the stream that helps cool the stifling heat of the day.

"I thought I'd spring a bit of a surprise on you! It's 1847, and I've brought you to meet Henry Rawlinson, who has just copied some rare Babylonian inscriptions from a perilous rock face. It has beaten all previous attempts by archaeologists as the ledge is so high up and very narrow."

"So how did the inscription writers make their marks in the first place?" asks Milton.

"Very good question – and I'm not sure we know! It must have involved ladders and nerves of steel. Even Rawlinson with his good head for heights had to rope in a local boy to do the very last part as it defeated even this experienced climber."

---

8 For the first visit to Baghdad, see *Rocky Road to Galileo*.

"So he has writing that no one has seen close up for thousands of years? What does he do next?"

"He now has the tricky task of translating an unknown language for which there is as yet no key."

"Is that him over there?" Milton gulps as he takes a good look at Rawlinson's companions. "Sitting in the shade with the mongoose, the lion, and the leopard?"

"Yes. He is something of an animal collector too. Best behaviour, Milton. We don't want to end up as supper."

"I think I can work out some of the kings' names," Rawlinson is saying to his pets. "Having these inscriptions repeated in more than one language means that we have found our equivalent of the Rosetta Stone, which unlocked the Egyptian hieroglyphs! Soon we will be able to read the works of the ancient Babylonians."

"This is all very interesting," whispers Milton. "But why does this matter to our quest?"

"It matters," says Harriet, "because it shows archaeology is making scientifically inspired strides, running controlled experiments in cracking the code of ancient languages in an alphabet called cuneiform – that means 'wedge-shaped.'"

Want to see some cuneiform? Here are Harriet's and Milton's initials in the script:

"Cool! That language looks a bit like fish bones!" says Milton.

"You would think that. I see them more as keys. Rawlinson joins a team of three other language experts sending in translations based on this code. The fact that four separate scholars come up with more or less the same translation shows they have read the code correctly. The key turns in the lock and the mysteries of the Babylonian culture are revealed! Let's go and paddle in the river for a moment."

Harriet leads Milton to a shady spot on the banks of the Tigris. Milton feels like he could be in almost any time in the last few thousand years, lying here, enjoying the sun with his friend.

"And what do they find with their key?" he asks lazily. "Instructions to locate golden treasures in pyramids of ancient kings, like in the movies with Indiana Jones or Lara Croft?"

"Better than that." Harriet nibbles on a leaf, remembering she'd missed out on her cactus snack some time ago.

"Mummies and cursed tombs?"

"Oh, there are plenty of archaeological expeditions that do that kind of thing too. But these men interested in the writing find lots of stories among the fragments, including one called *Gilgamesh*, a Mesopotamian epic poem that is possibly the oldest surviving work of literature. In my opinion, stories are our real treasures, as we can pass them down to the next generation and they never fade. Everyone can share them."

"That's true. So how did these fragments survive so long?"

"They were written on fragile clay tablets, which last better than paper. These had been dug up by archaeologists and sent back to the British Museum undeciphered. A man called George Smith was given the job of working his way through the fragments. His reaction to finding this particular fragment was most un-Victorian! Far from having an English reserved manner, he went into a full-scale football celebration, complete with casting off his shirt!"

I'VE FOUND IT!

"What had he found?" asks Milton eagerly. "Why was he so excited?"

"He'd found an account of the Flood, not from the Bible but in the epic poem. Until that time, very little had been known about the world in which the Old Testament was written. That, and fragments of other stories found at ancient sites, opened up the new idea for biblical studies that the early stories in the Bible were shared with other cultures around at the time."

"So they were the same stories?"

"Not the same. The Bible stories are very much their own history, told by a different set of people, using the same foundational tale."

Milton is even more curious now. "Who were they, these people?"

"The people of the Old Testament, the Jews, were in exile at the time in Babylon. The young scholars learned cuneiform and read ancient stories like *Gilgamesh* in their textbooks. They came across phrases in these old tales, like the animals going in two-by-two, so it seems likely they adapted these for their own purposes for the stories in the book we now call Genesis, or the first book in the Bible. That is the book that contains the story of Noah and the ark as well as Adam and Eve and the creation of the world. Perhaps they already had their own versions, but when they told them this time, they were casting them in the light of their belief in the Hebrew God."

"So why was George Smith so excited?"

"He and many others thought it might help to understand why the Bible came to be written in the version we now have; the writers meant to express their revolutionary big picture that a single good God – and not the quarrelling gods of the Babylonian world – made the world and sent the Flood."

"So scientific advances in archaeology, such as codebreaking and better excavations, had an impact on the big picture for religion and science?" suggests Milton.

"Yes – thanks to the excavations, the Victorians discovered when the idea of a lawgiver outside creation was first made clear in ancient writings."

"Cool!"

Harriet gets up, having eaten her fill. "We'd better get on with the quest. In answer to your question, Milton, not everyone reads the Bible in its historical context like this, but many Victorians found it encouraging to dig up so many traces of the similar stories – as well as evidence of the kings and high officials mentioned in the Bible."

"And what about the creation story, the one with Adam and Eve and the seven days of creation?"

"Yes, we must pay close attention to that one because it has been used for thousands of years by the religions who follow the Bible to shape our understanding of the physical universe. There were other stories found about creation too in ancient Babylon, but the Genesis account took its own path here as well. It helps to understand where it came from, which is most likely to be some writers in Babylonian exile putting their own stories in circulation to keep Jewish culture alive and well."

Milton is puzzled. "So does that mean that Adam and Eve – and the Flood – are just stories?"

"That's for you to decide, as science can't tell us all the answers."

"But I want to know if they are true!"

"I can tell you that it's a very old debate. The best way to answer this is to say that there is a spectrum of views on this among faith groups. Some people believe the stories literally. A few have even spent years looking for physical traces of Noah's ark. In the middle are people who see them as stories that contain a memory of some historical event, shaped by later retellings, but perhaps not a blow-by-blow account. Many people see them as stories that help us to understand why God created the world and humankind but aren't trying to give a literal account of what happened.

"Remember back in sixth-century Alexandria? Philoponus said that he thought Genesis pointed to the fact of God's creation, not how it came about. In the early seventeenth century, Galileo said that the Bible talks about how to go to heaven and not how heaven goes. This was the stance many Christians decided to take."

"And what do you think?"

"That maybe we need to work out what kind of knowledge these stories are trying to give us – and these archaeological discoveries certainly help with that. What about you?"

"I think it is all very curious!"

They have arrived back at the time machine. They can see Rawlinson patting his leopard on the head.

"Do you think it might be approaching dinner time?" asks Milton as his tummy rumbles.

"For you or the leopard?" asks Harriet.

The next thing she sees is the tip of Milton's tale disappearing inside the box.

All Aboard the Express Train! Meet the Engineers

"I think it is time to check in on what the Industrial Revolution is doing before we visit any more scientists," says Harriet. "I've prepared you a second timeline for the advances in chemistry, physics, and engineering – all of which are helping each other."

Harriet's Timeline of Top 19th-Century Discoveries: Part 2

PHYSICS, CHEMISTRY, AND ENGINEERING

1805 John Dalton's atomic theory

1816 First working telegraph installed over short distance in London suburb; by 1866 there is a working system across the Atlantic, and by 1902 one circling the world

1820 Hans Christian Ørsted finds a relationship between electricity and magnetism

1825 First public railway opens: the Stockton and Darlington railway

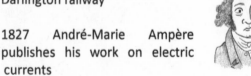

1827 André-Marie Ampère publishes his work on electric currents

1831 Michael Faraday discovers electromagnetic induction

1846 Astronomers discover Neptune, based on prediction by the French mathematician Urbain Le Verrier

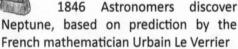

1854 Lord Kelvin defines the field of thermodynamics, the reaction of heat to forces and electrical current

1864 James Clerk Maxwell's theory of electromagnetism

1869 Dmitri Mendeleev establishes the first Periodic Table

1879 Thomas Edison makes first successful test of electric light bulb

1895 Wilhelm Röntgen discovers X-rays

1896 Henri Becquerel discovers radioactivity

1898 J. J. Thomson proposes Plum Pudding model of an atom

1898 Marie Curie discovers polonium and radium, and coins term "radioactivity"

1900 Max Planck's law of black body radiation, which becomes basis for quantum theory

Milton looks a bit worried. "I don't understand some of these technical words."

"Don't be anxious. It is true that science is getting more specialized in this century with more difficult terms, but we'll visit the scientists and they'll explain the ones you need to know. But first we are going to see something you'll have no trouble understanding: science in action!"

"Hooray! I always like a bit of action!" Milton chases his tail.

"The nineteenth century is the great time for applying science in Britain and around the world. America, Germany, France – all are racing away to have the most developed industries. And the people leading the charge are the engineers."

Milton stops suddenly and yawns. "Applied science? Engineers? That sounds boring!"

"What if I said that it means steam trains, steam ships, photography, cinema, aeroplanes, and cars?"

Milton leaps to his paws again. "I'd say all aboard!"

Harriet laughs as she sets the time machine down on a grassy hillside in Wiltshire, England. "I thought you'd like to visit one of this century's greatest engineering achievements, built by the man who surely has the best name of the period."

ISAMBARD KINGDOM BRUNEL

"You're right: that is a cool name, and a very unusual hat choice."

"I did think of taking you to see Brunel build the first tunnel under the Thames in 1828, but as he almost died in a flooding accident, that might be a bit scary. Then there is his suspension bridge in Bristol, but he didn't live to see that completed. I thought you might prefer this tunnel through Box Hill – the longest railway tunnel of its day at 1.83 miles[9] – as part of the Great Western railway he was building from London to Exeter. We are here for the opening in June 1841."

They arrive breathless at Bath station. Milton is humming with excitement.

"Oh, Harriet – this is the best adventure yet!"

"Just wait until we fly to the moon on Apollo 11. Mind you, I think a railway ride must have felt very similar to Victorians. Until now they've been limited by the speed of the fastest horse.

---

9 2.95 kilometres.

Now they have a steam engine. The fastest steam train will reach 126 miles per hour[10] in the next century – that's a lot faster than most trains you can go on in our time."

"Are there other engineers with a need for speed at this time?"

"Why don't you find out?"

TRY THIS AT HOME: BUILD LIKE A VICTORIAN ENGINEER

Engineers often have to put up buildings in places with challenging conditions. Can you build a structure that would withstand an earthquake? You will need only three things to test this:

- A packet of dry spaghetti
- A packet of marshmallows
- Your imagination!

You might like to look first online to see the basic steel or wooden frame structures of famous buildings: the Eiffel Tower, a pagoda, a skyscraper.

Now build a model from the spaghetti, using the marshmallows as joints. They hold your structure together.

Once you are happy with what you've built, wobble the table top gently. Does your structure stay standing? If not, how did it fall over? Does that give you an idea of how to improve the design?[11]

Can it hold a load? Pile the remaining marshmallows on top and see what happens!

---

10   203 kilometres per hour.
11   You can get a good scientific explanation to help you here from Howcast: https://www.youtube.com/watch?v=y6FmrOS72EA

Back in the time machine, Milton presents Harriet with his list.

"I've done my research," he says, twitching his whiskers. "I found out that engineers not only build big things like bridges, but also small things, like electric light bulbs and motors."

"That's right. Engineering has lots of different branches, or specializations; even more in our time," says Harriet. "And this time machine was built by one in our future."

MILTON'S LIST OF TOP TEN ENGINEERS (NOT INCLUDING IKB!)

1. Thomas Telford (1757–1834) – fast forward to the future! Road, bridge, and canal builder

2. Richard Trevithick (1771–1833) – on the right track, Builder of first steam-powered railway in 1804

3. George Stephenson (1781–1848) and his son Robert (1803–59) – rocket men! Builder of public railways and the famous Rocket locomotive

4. Thomas Brassey (1805–70) – full steam ahead! Builder of one in every twenty miles of the world's railways by the time of his death

5. Gustave Eiffel (1832–1923) – a race to the top. Engineer behind the Eiffel Tower, the tallest building in the world at the time

6. Nikolaus Otto (1832–91) – go faster. Inventor of four-stroke petrol engine

7. Emily Warren Roebling (1843–1903) – first female field engineer. Oversaw completion of Brooklyn Bridge

8. Alexander Graham Bell (1847–1922) – speedy communications. Inventor of the telephone

9. Thomas Edison (1847–1931) – light touch. Inventor of the modern age with his light bulb, sound recording, and motion picture camera

10. Nikola Tesla (1856–1943) – speedy power. Electrical engineer, designed modern alternating current power supply

"These are all excellent suggestions," says Harriet. "But what about the even more important engineers?"

Milton is a bit miffed. He thinks he's included everyone he should. "Like who?"

"Like the ones who cured London's Great Stink in 1858."

"Great Stink? Harriet, is this going to be a smelly adventure?"

"Very, I'm afraid."

She opens the door of the time machine to reveal a dark brick-lined tunnel. It is too small to be a railway and has water running along the bottom.

"Where are we?" asks Milton. He's not sure he wants to step out into the river. *How deep is it?* he wonders.

"Under London. Over there is arguably the most important civil engineer of them all at this time, Joseph Bazalgette. Come on: this is nothing that another shower won't wash off."

The two time travellers wade gingerly through the muddy water. Milton is really not keen on a few of Harriet's recent choices of places to visit. The apple orchards and Greek theatres were much more fun.

"I suppose it is good to see that applied science isn't all about fast trains and electric lights," says Milton, trying to make the best of this part of the adventure.

"That's why I brought our quest here. A few years ago in a very hot summer the Thames got so smelly with sewage that central London was both stinky and dangerous, as many people died from waterborne diseases. The British Houses of Parliament are built right on the Thames and so the men in power got a full blast of the smell. Not surprising then that they quickly set their best engineers to solving the problem."

They stand a few paces away from Bazalgette, who is checking the progress on the tunnels.

"Excellent work. When we connect these up, the Thames should return to its former condition. Maybe one day we'll be able to fish in it again?" says Bazalgette. "It used to have trout and salmon once upon a time."

"You'd only fish out old boots and much worse at the moment," grumbles the workman. "Well, I'd better get on, sir. Can't have another summer like the Great Stink, can we?"

"Very true." The engineer wades to the next archway to carry out his inspection.

"Joseph Bazalgette here is building new pumping stations and miles of new sewers, and that solves the problem," says Harriet. "His system is so well built that it is still in use in our time. He probably saved more lives than any other Londoner of his day." She turns to head back to the time machine. "And that leads me to another area of science we mustn't neglect: medicine! For this, I'm afraid, we're heading into a war zone."

Milton thinks Harriet sounds strangely eager, but he too is pleased to get out of the sewer.

"I'm not sure that going to war is going to be any better than going down a sewer. You really want to make me understand that science isn't all about laboratories, don't you?"

"How did you guess?" says Harriet with a smile.

The Lady with the Lamp

Milton is first out of the time machine, to prove he isn't a scaredy-cat. "I can't hear any guns," he says, keeping his voice low. In fact, the chamber he has walked into is dark and quiet apart from a few snores and an occasional groan from the men lying in the camp beds along the walls.

"We're at a nursing station in Scutari, Turkey, in 1854. The fighting is some miles away in a place called the Crimea on the Black Sea," explains Harriet. "British soldiers hurt in the conflict are sent here. A short while ago, before the person we've come to see arrived, they were left in very dirty conditions and many died from infections. The press reported this and the British government knew it had to do something."

"I think I know who we are going to meet – it's Florence Nightingale, isn't it?"

"Yes, known to the patients as 'the lady with the lamp'. She was sent out here to head a team of nurses. And here she is now." Harriet points to a woman coming down the space between the beds to check all is well.

"She does more than just offer comfort. She improves hygiene and keeps information on food, death rates, and doctors' training so that when she comes home she writes a book called *Notes on Nursing*, which is still in print today. She is the founder of modern good nursing practices."

"I've never thought of her as a scientist," admits Milton.

Harriet counts her points off on her claws. "She observes the conditions, collects data, and writes up her conclusions. This won her a place as the first female member of the Royal Statistical Society, so she is a mathematician as well as a nursing pioneer."

"So not just a lady with a lamp." Milton watches as Florence offers a wounded man a cup of water. It is miserable to be injured in war, but at least these soldiers are getting the best care available at the time.

"Definitely not!" Harriet says quickly. "Her work is part of a wider movement that revolutionizes medicine. To understand that, I think we need to go and look at another pump."

Milton has learned his lesson. "Not down a mine – or a sewer?"

"No. Above ground and in the city of London in 1854."

Milton is still suspicious. He watches the wards of Scutari melt away and be replaced by the packed houses of Soho in the heart of old London. It looks safe enough.

Harriet opens the door just as a shire horse clatters by pulling a wagon of beer barrels. "Mind your step and don't drink anything."

The two time travellers watch a crowd of women chatting and filling buckets at the water pump in Broad Street. Their small children hang on their skirts while older ones play with hoops or leapfrog over each other. A man in a dark suit is interviewing them, taking notes.

"I guess we've come to see that man?" asks Milton. "He looks the scientific sort."

"Yes. He's called John Snow. There has been a cholera outbreak and by talking to the families who have lost loved ones, he has worked out that this pump is the source."

"This pump!" Milton looks set to run into the crowd of women and warn them against using it. Harriet pulls him back.

"We can't. We'd change the timeline. John Snow has to be the one to point this out – which he has – and here is the council man now."

A worker turns up with a big spanner. "Right, ladies, find another pump and pour your buckets away. This one is out of order." He takes off the handle so it can no longer be used.

"But I'll have to walk miles to get water now!" grumbles one mother.

"At least you'll be alive to do so," says the man, taking the handle with him. "Listen to the doctor: he makes a good case about the harm done by dirty water."

Milton relaxes. "I knew you wouldn't bring me to see them suffer. So John Snow changes people's big picture of how diseases are transmitted?"

"He does, like our friend Professor Acland in Oxford. But the idea that disease is transmitted in dirty water is given a fuller scientific hearing when a Frenchman called Louis Pasteur comes up with germ theory as a result of experiments between 1860 and 1864. He suggests microorganisms carry germs, rather than the old miasma theory that disease is carried in bad air. Thanks to the microscope work of earlier scientists, people are more ready to believe in something they can't see with the naked eye or smell."

Milton is having another great thought. "Pasteur? Don't we drink *pasteurized* milk?"

"We do – and it is named after him. It's a way of processing milk to kill the germs without spoiling the taste."

Milton licks his lips. "I think I have a new hero!"

A Shocking Adventure!
Faraday and Maxwell

"Let's move on from biological sciences," announces Harriet. "There is so much science to fit in this century that we've got to make time for physics."

"Harriet, we're in a time machine," says Milton in a superior tone. "Time is not our problem."

She smiles. "That's good, because we are going back a few years to 1832. As a bit of background, I should mention that electricity is coming on in leaps and bounds."

MEET THE FIRST SCIENTIFIC MONSTER: FRANKENSTEIN'S CREATURE

We can't get very far into the history of electricity without dropping in on the first science-fiction writer who uses it to electrifying effect! Mary Shelley, at only eighteen, was challenged one stormy summer in 1816 to come up with a ghost story. She in fact came up with something much more interesting: a novel about a scientist creating a creature out of scavenged body parts and using a mixture of alchemy and electricity to create life. All does not go well when the scientist, Victor Frankenstein, rejects his creation and the creature goes on the rampage.

It's a brilliant scientific novel showing the dangers of letting your experiments get out of hand. It also tells us not to be too ambitious and consider the consequences... and it was all thought up by a teenager.

"After the early days of experiments with batteries and lightning conductors,[12] in 1820 a Danish scientist called Hans Christian Ørsted discovered a link between electricity and magnetism, and many have been exploring this new area. We are going to meet the leading public scientist of the day, Michael Faraday. He is about to give a lecture explaining an exciting new discovery he has made about electromagnetic induction."

Milton doesn't like it when Harriet springs long words on him so shows his displeasure by cleaning his fur.

"Don't worry, Milton. You'll understand in a moment because Mr Faraday is about to explain it at a meeting in the Royal Institution in London. But we'd better hurry if we want good seats.

---

12   See *Hunt with Newton* for more details.

ELECTROMAGNETIC INDUCTION

This is a battery connected to a small coil of wire.

Over here is a large coil connected to a meter – no current is showing.

Now I slide the small one in and out of the large one and look – !

Shocking – a current has been induced!

"Can you see what he did?" whispers Harriet. "He induced, or made, an electric current in the larger coil by bringing the magnetic field of the smaller one very close. He uses this idea later to develop a dynamo and an electric motor."

Milton and Harriet follow the crowd into the Royal Institution library, where the people gather around the tables set out with interesting scientific exhibits for them to examine and discuss.

"I'm still not sure I understand, Harriet," says Milton. "Why does magnetism produce an electric current?"

Harriet scuttles under a table to avoid being trodden on. "Faraday thinks of electricity and magnetism as different forms of the same force. He also comes up with the idea of a field for that force. Remember that, because it is going to be essential to twentieth-century physics."

"A force field? Like in *Star Wars*?" Milton does his best Jedi knight impression.

"Not that sort! A scientific one." Harriet rolls her eyes. "We are used to the idea now but at the time Faraday was painting a new picture of how things work in the universe."

"I'm not sure I know what a force field is outside of science fiction."

"I'll try to explain." Harriet looks around her for inspiration. "You can't see force fields, only detect them. Look at all these people circling this table in the same direction, held by their attraction to the objects on display. That is a little like a magnetic field around a wire through which you run a current. The further off, the less strong the attraction. Faraday himself used the picture of flowing liquid so people could visualize what he meant."

TRY THIS AT HOME: FEEL THE ATTRACTION!

You can't see magnetic fields (though birds might!), but you can do experiments to detect them. You might be able at school to experiment with iron filings to make patterns like this:

But here is an experiment you can do safely at home. You'll need two fairly strong magnets and some spare household nails or pins. Set everything out on paper on a tray.

Not sure you have any magnets? Don't forget to look in the toy box – some toy trains are linked by magnets and there are some construction games that use them. You might also have fridge magnets. These aren't as strong but you'll still be able to do the first part of the test.

1. First try and push the magnets together. Can you feel the attraction and repulsion between them? That's because they have a north and south pole. Two like poles don't like to be together!

2. How near does a nail have to be to the magnet to be attracted? It should swing around to point or even move towards the magnet. Mark the spot in pencil and keep moving the nail to new positions to see if this changes.

3. What pattern do you see? Are there places where the attraction is stronger than others?

"Faraday sounds a very clever man," says Milton.

"He is, especially when you think that he started out with many disadvantages. Like Mary Anning, he was very poor. His father was a blacksmith and Faraday himself was an apprentice bookbinder – not the usual background for a scientist at the time. He also belongs to a strict Christian group called the Sandemanians. He remains a member until his death, which set him a little apart all his life from his scientific colleagues. His persistence, however, got him noticed by Humphry Davy, the inventor of the safety lamp. Davy found him a job here at the Royal Institution, and Faraday is now a scientific star, loved for the clear way he demonstrates his discoveries to the public. He also started lectures in 1826 for children – probably the first scientist to do this."

"I like the fact that there are so many women in the audience for his talk as well," says Milton. "It looks like the kinds of people who are involved in science is changing after years of being only for wealthy men!"

"He respects women's contribution to science. He says he owes much of his early education to a writer on chemistry called Jane Marcet. He makes sure she gets free entry whenever she comes to the institution."

The room is now emptying and they are able to get close enough to Faraday to hear him talking with a female guest.

"Sir," asks the lady, "do you worry that what you are discovering is going to conflict with your faith?"

"No, madam," he says as he packs away his electrical equipment. "I don't, for nothing in the works of God can contradict the higher things that belong to faith. The things I discover in nature show me the wisdom and power of God in creation. Still, I do not think it at all necessary to tie the study of natural sciences and religion together, do you? Each have their own place in our lives."

Milton and Harriet tiptoe back to the time machine.

MEET THE FEMALE SCIENTISTS!

While Harriet and Milton head off to the next stop in their quest, we are going to meet some of the women in the middle of the nineteenth century who made their mark on Victorian science. The door was just opening to women and there were a few (in addition to Caroline Herschel and Mary Anning) who managed to push their way inside against the odds!

MARY SOMERVILLE: THE QUEEN OF SCIENCE

- Lived: 1780–1872
- Number of jobs: 2 (mathematician and science writer on many subjects – in addition to being a wife and mother. Her first husband stopped her studying; the second encouraged her)
- Influence (out of 100): 56 (as a self-taught mathematician, she won a medal for solving mathematical problems and published papers on light and magnetism but was most influential for her scientific writing. She translated from French Pierre-Simon Laplace's *The Mechanism of the Heavens* and went on to write her own book, *The Connexion of the Physical Sciences*, in which she makes the important observation that research of late had led to the simplifying of the laws of nature and uniting detached branches by general principles. She also wrote the bestselling *Physical Geography*, the first English book on the subject. She had a direct influence on both mathematician Ada Lovelace and physicist James Clerk Maxwell, whom Harriet and Milton will meet next)
- Right? (out of 20): 18 (we now think of four basic forces controlling the interactions between everything from subatomic[13] particles to stars in galaxies)
- Helpfully wrong? (out of 10): 0 (not often wrong)
- Interesting fact: we have the term "scientist" due to her. The man who coined the word, William Whewell, used it about her as "man of science" clearly didn't fit. It was then entered in the *Oxford English Dictionary* that same year. She also has an Oxford college named after her. Her face appears on Scottish £10 banknotes.

---

13   "Subatomic" means the particles that make up atoms, like electrons.

MARY SOMERVILLE

On the banknote: 34120 · The Royal Bank of Scotland plc · TEN POUNDS STERLING · 34120 · £10 · £10

ADA, COUNTESS OF LOVELACE: THE FIRST COMPUTER PROGRAMMER

- Lived: 1815–52
- Number of jobs: 1 (mathematician – she was also best known in her day as the daughter of Lord Byron, a very famous poet)
- Influence (out of 100): 35 (her influence was to come long after her death, but she was the first to recognize that Charles Babbage's Analytical Engine, an early form of calculator, could be used for tasks beyond calculation. Her greatest achievement was to devise an algorithm intended for the machine, which earns her the title of first computer programmer)
- Right? (out of 20): 10 (she was right to see computers could be used for so much more but was hampered by the fact Babbage's machine had to wait to be built until 2002 to test her algorithm)
- Helpfully wrong? (out of 10): 2 (like her contemporaries, she was also a supporter of the pseudosciences of phrenology (the study of skulls as an

indicator of character) and mesmerism (an early form of hypnosis), neither of which were very productive scientific areas)

• Interesting fact? Mary Somerville was her maths tutor – a very lucky break for a gifted child!

ADA, COUNTESS OF LOVELACE

ELIZABETH GARRETT ANDERSON: THE DOCTOR WILL SEE YOU NOW

• Lived: 1836–1917
• Number of jobs: 4 (doctor, founder of hospital and medical school for women, mayor, magistrate)
• Influence (out of 100): 92 (at a time when men only were allowed to be doctors, Elizabeth found a loophole in the Society of Apothecaries' rules to become the first woman openly[14] to obtain a medical qualification.

---

14   We know of one who did so as a man – James Miranda Barry (1795–1865) started life being raised as a female and spent the years after twenty living as a man and working as a doctor. His birth sex was only revealed after his death.

She went on to found a hospital for women and children, as well as open a college where women could train in medicine – thus opening up the career path for girls)

- Right? (out of 20): 20 (she changed in both argument and by example the unhealthy lifestyle most women were condemned to in Victorian society and paved the way for a more equal educational path)
- Helpfully wrong? (out of 10): 0 (she got things right!)
- Interesting fact: she added to her firsts: first dean of a medical school, first woman on a school board, and first female mayor and magistrate – go Elizabeth!

BRAVO!

HURRAH!

ELIZABETH GARRETT ANDERSON

What's the go o' that?

The time machine lands in a familiar city of spires and gardens. Milton pokes his head outside the door.

"I know where we are: we're back in Cambridge!"

"That's right. The year is 1856 and we are here to meet one of the greatest Scotsmen – and one of the greatest scientists – who has ever lived."

Milton racks his brains for a name. He has a gap in his greatest scientist list between Darwin and Einstein. "I give up. Who is it?"

"His name is James Clerk Maxwell, and I've brought you to meet him when he is still quite a young man, only twenty-four. He's just about to make two very interesting discoveries in astronomy and in optics – and these aren't even his best work."

Milton isn't sure if he's going to like such a clever clogs. He sounds more like Harriet's kind of person. "Maybe we should skip this visit and you can just tell me about him?"

"Oh no, you'll like him," says Harriet.

"He sounds as if he's going to be very big-headed."

"Far from it – his father made sure of that when he designed his schoolboy son a special suit of clothes!"

"I want to meet the boy who survived that!" agrees Milton.

"Oh, by the way," says Harriet, beetling along fast for a tortoise, "I also live in Cambridge at this time. We'd better hope I've not escaped the Darwins' garden."

Milton runs after her. "Harriet!"

They enter Trinity College, which hasn't changed much since they last chased Newton through the quad. Harriet takes Milton to Maxwell's, room where the young fellow of the college is muttering to himself. They hide in the folds of the curtains to spy on what he is doing.

"The rings of Saturn. Now what's the go o' that?" the young man murmurs.

"I see he likes 'how' questions," whispers Milton.

"He is also committed to the 'why' ones too. He is part of a discussion group called the Cambridge Apostles and takes his Christian faith very seriously all during his life, able to quote huge amounts of the Bible. In fact, he said his faith released him to fly to the ends of the earth with his questions and find out formulas to describe accurately how the real world works."

"To find what's the go o' that," says Milton.

"You've got a terrible Scottish accent," comments Harriet. "Now let's watch."

"Looking at the mathematical models, I conclude that the rings of Saturn can be neither solid like a wedding ring, nor made up of a fluid. The rings must be like a flight of brickbats," says Maxwell, juggling with some pebbles on his desk.

Harriet nudges Milton. "See! He goes on from here to work out later in 1856 while living in Aberdeen that the rings of Saturn are made up of lots of rocks held in orbit – something that was only finally confirmed in the 1980s when the space probes Voyager 1 and 2 made a fly-by and sent back images to earth."

"And he did that with maths?" Milton is impressed. He already likes maths and now he has even more reason to carry on with his studies: it could take him to outer space!

Maxwell leans back in his chair having completed his scientific paper and looks up at the ceiling. "Wouldn't it be wonderful to see that for oneself? Ah! That reminds me." He gets out another notebook. "Thomas Young suggested that the human eye might have three colour receptors. In the little experiment with my colour wheel yesterday, I think he may be right on the number, but the receptors are red, green, and blue."

TRY THIS AT HOME: MAXWELL'S COLOUR WHEEL

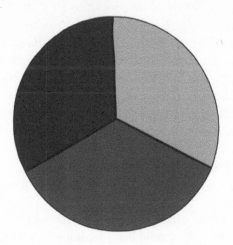

Based on Newton's colour spectrum, which split white light, Thomas Young thought that mixing on a spinning top, the primary colours – red, blue, and yellow – might be perceived as white by the eye. Maxwell tested this and found it wasn't the case. He tried different combinations – you can too. He found that the combination to produce white is, in fact, red, blue, and green.

1. Draw around a side plate on white card.

2. Cut out the circle and divide into three equal segments (you can measure angles from the centre of 120° to get this spot on).

3. Paint each segment red, blue, and green. Use mid shades from your poster paints to be as close to the primary colour as you can get. Let this dry.

4. Pierce the card at the centre carefully with a sharpened pencil.

5. Spin as fast as you can like a spinning top. What colour does your eye see if looking directly down at it?

Why do three different shades produce one colour? The answer is that there is a slight delay between seeing and processing what we see, which allows for colours spinning very fast to merge in our brain. That produces the combined colour of white.

You can now try other colour combinations and see what your eye perceives. For example, what about just yellow and blue?[15]

15   The answer is pink. Maxwell did the same test and this led him to work out the difference between additive and subtractive colour mixing – something every artist needs to understand!

Harriet coaxes Milton away as he has got distracted chasing a rainbow of light cast by a crystal hanging at the window. It looks very like the one they bought with Newton two hundred years ago. Surely not...? Fortunately Maxwell is so deep in his work that he doesn't notice the leaps and miaows of an excited cat.

Back in the time machine, Harriet resets the dial. "There is so much I could show you in Maxwell's short life. He makes many fascinating discoveries in physics and maths, often assisted by his wife, Katherine, but perhaps we should visit him next at church in London. He is now a professor at King's College."

"Church? What's that got to do with science?" asks Milton.

"It's the building itself that gives him his next great step forward – specifically the belfry."

"My dear," says Maxwell, "I've had an idea."

"You are never short of those, James," his wife teases.

"I know – and I thank you for putting up with me. But is it not wonderful that humankind's reason should be made a judge over God's works, and should measure, weigh, and calculate – so that we can say at last that 'I understand – I have discovered – it is right and true!'"

"Indeed, it is, James. So what is your idea?" She twirls her parasol, narrowly avoiding hitting Milton, who has crept too close.

"I've been thinking about electromagnetism, such as the work done by Mr Faraday. I have come up with some equations that unify light, electricity, and magnetism and show them as all signs of the same phenomenon."

"My dear, that is wonderful!" exclaims Katherine.

"The issue is, I'm not exactly sure how the figures I input end up with the right outputs – but I've now realized that doesn't matter. Look at the belfry. As long as we know which rope to pull to produce the toll of which bell, we don't need to know the mechanism inside the tower. We can put in our numbers and out comes a reliable result."

"It sounds, my dear, that you have come up with a new method: leap over the unknown to arrive at mathematically workable knowledge!"

"My belfry.[16] I'm comforted that I am right because the more physical science advances, the more we see that the laws of nature are not mere arbitrary and unconnected decisions of God; they are essential parts of one universal system."

"You are saying that thanks to knowing the inputs and the outputs are correct, we can trust the processes taking place in the belfry?"

"Exactly, my dear. And I find that thinking that leaves God out of the picture is unworkable, so we'd better hurry inside."

The two Maxwells carry on into church for the service.

---

16   This method of thinking is now often called a "black box".

"So what are these equations he has thought up?" asks Milton.

"Remember the basic experiment we saw Faraday perform? Maxwell's equations unify electricity and magnetism, and show how light is an electromagnetic wave. Every electrical device you can think of depends on them."

"Wow! And I'd never heard of him!"

"That's partly because he dies young at only forty-eight of cancer, his life not long enough for his reputation to be firmly set in people's minds. Rather like with Mary Anning, other people sometimes reap the rewards. He packed a lot in, though, including developing the Cavendish Laboratory, where our quest started. The words over the door were put there by him and reflect his big picture of how faith and science fit together."

"So Maxwell was forgotten?"

"Not forgotten. He was very well known to those that needed to know him for their own work. Albert Einstein kept a picture of him on his desk and called Maxwell the end and beginning of an epoch in science. Richard Feynman, a quantum physicist of the next century, said that in the long view – he meant ten thousand years – the most significant event of the nineteenth century will be Maxwell's discovery of the laws of electrodynamics."

"So we can say that he did find 'the go o' that' for our modern age?"

"He certainly did. So what next?"

Milton chases a butterfly for a few minutes.

Harriet gets tired of waiting. "Milton?"

He pauses, tail kinked with happiness. "Did you know that someone once said that a butterfly flapping its wings can cause a typhoon somewhere else?"

"Ah, so you were doing scientific research into non-linear impacts?"

"If you say so. I thought I was just playing."

"I think, Milton, that you are ready for the twentieth and twenty-first centuries. Let's go to the atomic age!"

Milton waves his tail goodbye to the butterfly and they get back into the time machine. Harriet punches in the coordinates to spin forward a few decades.

"Put these on first before you get out," says Harriet, handing Milton a yellow hazmat suit. "We're in Paris and things are about to go radioactive."

Harriet leads Milton to a window in a laboratory door. A woman in a black dress is standing at a bench running an experiment.

"I know her!" says Milton excitedly. "That's Marie Skłodowska-Curie, the first woman to win Nobel Prizes for both physics and chemistry!"

"That's right, Milton. Science has voyaged far from the beginning of the century. By the end, who is doing science, and what they are studying have changed. Do you want to meet her?"

"Oh yes!"

They open the door and walk in...

To be continued in Harriet and Milton's final adventure: *Modern Flights*!

Where to go to find out more

Dinosaurs

If you want to find out more about Mary Anning and other dinosaur hunters, there are many excellent places to visit. Have a look in your local museum to see if they have any fossils. If you can visit London, go to the Natural History Museum, which has a special exhibition about her. You can also look at it on their website: **http://www.nhm.ac.uk/discover/mary-anning-unsung-hero.html**

And if you are in Dorset (also in the UK), you could visit Lyme Regis. There are two museums featuring fossils and, best of all, the beach where Mary found her samples. But please remember the safety tips and keep away from the cliffs! If that's too far for you, find out if your local area has revealed any interesting finds. There's a global map here to find out more: **https://paleobiodb.org/navigator**

Charles Darwin

You can find lots more information about Charles Darwin in books and online. We enjoyed the information about the *Beagle* voyage found here: **http://darwin-online.org.uk/BeagleLibrary/Beagle_Library_Introduction.htm**
For information on how to use the biologist's tool, a quadrat, go to **http://www.bbc.co.uk/bitesize/standard/biology/biosphere/investigating_an_ecosystem/revision/2**

Michael Faraday

Interested in Michael Faraday? You can see his laboratory and the space where he gave his lectures if you visit the Royal Institution, London. Their museum also has Davy lamps and many other fascinating objects from Victorian science. You can also see his laboratory on the website: **http://www.rigb.org/our-history/michael-faraday**

James Clerk Maxwell

Want to see the colour wheel in action? Here's a good video: **https://www.bbc.co.uk/programmes/p03q39zr**

Answers

How many times did you spot the Curiosity Bug? The answer is 20.

Thanks

Julia is grateful to the writers Deborah Cadbury (*The Dinosaur Hunters*), James Hamilton (*Faraday: The Life*), and Patricia Pierce (*Jurassic Mary*).

Meet the authors

Julia Golding is a multi-award-winning children's novelist, including the *Cat Royal* series and the *Companions Quartet*. Having given up on science at sixteen, she became interested again when she realized just how inspiring science can be. It really does tell the best stories! This is her first experiment with non-fiction but hopefully her collaborators, Roger and Andrew, will prevent any laboratory accidents.

Andrew Briggs is the professor of nanomaterials at the University of Oxford. Nanomaterials just means small stuff. In his laboratory he studies problems like how electricity flows through a single molecule (you can't get stuff much smaller than a single molecule). He is also curious about big questions. He flies aeroplanes, but he has never been in a time travel machine like the one that Harriet and Milton use – yet!

Roger Wagner is an artist who paints power stations and angels (among other things) and has work in collections around the world. He didn't do the drawings for these books, but like Milton and Harriet he wanted to find out how the 'big picture' thinking of artists was connected to what scientists do. When he met Andrew Briggs the two of them set out on a journey to answer that question. Their journey (which they described in a book called *The Penultimate Curiosity*), was almost (but not quite) as exciting as Milton and Harriet's.

Harriet and Milton continue
their quest in

MODERN
FLIGHTS
– available now!